Birds in the City

poems by

Jennifer L. Brinkley

Finishing Line Press
Georgetown, Kentucky

Birds in the City

ACKNOWLEDGMENTS

Thank you to the following journals and magazines for first publishing
versions of these poems:

To Have and to Hold (poetry). *Nebo Literary Journal*
On a June Night in 2000 (poetry). *Pink Panther Magazine*
Unraveling (poetry). Route 7 Review
A Mother's Love (poetry), Keeper of Things (poetry). In The Notebook: a
progressive journal about women & girls with rural & small town roots
Earth and Breath (poetry), Life Lessons (poetry). *In Still Here: VLP
Magazine.*
Dripping (poetry). *In Handful of Dust Magazine*
Homecoming (poetry). In *The Blue Pen Literary Magazine*
Threads (poetry). In *issue.Zero Literary Magazine*

Publisher: Leah Huete de Maines
Editor: Christen Kincaid
Cover Art: Old Town Sarajevo II by Yvonne Petkus, www.yvonnepetkus.com,
          Commissioned by Dr. David Lee
Author Photo: David S. Brinkley
Cover Design: Elizabeth Maines McCleavy

Order online: www.finishinglinepress.com
          also available on amazon.com

Author inquiries and mail orders:
Finishing Line Press
PO Box 1626
Georgetown, Kentucky 40324
USA

Table of Contents

For my father and mother,
Larry and Linda Belcher.
Thank you for teaching me the
importance of education and service.

Unraveling

We were strung like this fragile strand of pearls.
I guess it was always destined to break.
To fall to the floor, a hollow clatter,
An echo of days wasted, of words said and unsaid.
I drop to my knees to try to collect them
But they have already scattered
To the four corners of this space.
I do not have the energy to stand back up
So, I will just sit amongst them.
My fingers search for a smooth sphere.
Just one, if I could find just one smooth pearl in this dimming light.
Instead, my touch seems to find only jagged edges.
Unkind thoughts and harsh words spewed in anger.
Thoughtless actions, doors slammed, children crying.
How hard would it have been to be gentle?
To have bitten my tongue, to have turned my head?
Even the strongest rope unravels over time.
But we were never strong, were we?
At best we were like this thin thread I am holding.
Now it is left without its beauty.
I wanted you to wear this, but you tucked it away.
"To save for special occasions," you said.
I never once saw it around your neck.
Guess I didn't make our life too special.
The kids drove me home after the service.
There wasn't much to say, they had to get home to their own babies.
They made sure I had something to eat, tidied up the house.
You taught them well.
I'm not sure what I taught them all these years.
I tried for a while but then it just became too easy to stop trying.
To let you carry the weight. To watch you from the sidelines.
Now here I sit, too old to play in the game.
I am left without my beauty.
Like this lifeless string in my hands.

Weight

What weighs more…
The love of a mother
Or the love of a wife?
They are like competing vines—
        S t r e t c h i n g for footholds
        R e a c h i n g for higher ground—
Strangling the tree beneath.

Purple

You both were wearing purple.
I thought it strange that we were sharing a meal with Senator
Elizabeth Warren but who am I to
Question the logic of dreams?
Servers were running past our table,
Silverware clattering, glass tinkering.
How long had you known the Senator without telling me?
I sighed and added it to the list of questions standing between us.
You both were talking excitedly about
Projects and taxes and social contracts.
I listened, wondering why I had not worn purple.
Then he appeared, in that suit jacket he always wore.
Black checkered print, tie too tight, smile bright.
He said hello to the Senator and to my mother.
I sat frozen.
For years, I have wanted to dream about him.
Wanted to hug him in my sleep.
Wanted to say things I should have said on our last day.
The few times he has appeared there have been no words exchanged.
Yet here he was. Approaching, talking, breathing.
And I was the one who could not move. Could not speak.
Could not breathe.
I turned my head to the side and quietly asked Senator Warren,
"Can you see him, too?"
She looked me in the eyes and said,
"Anyone who loves him can still see him."
I rose and threw my arms around his neck.
And for a moment, before sleep disappeared,
I could feel his heartbeat.

Threads

I am from bright orange cotton and someone else's socks.
Itchy and ill-fitting.
Papers that say I'm no longer a mama.
Scars in places that say otherwise.

I am from doubters and low expectations.
Waiting for the first day of the month.
Stomachs empty by the fifteenth.
Peeled labels and broken glass.

I am from colored lights and late nights.
Men wanting things from me.
Me wanting things I can't afford.
Us meeting somewhere in the middle.

I am from switches and cigarette burns.
Sleeping with my hand between my legs.
Cracks of light when the door opens.
"No" and "Don't" heard only by a popcorn ceiling.

I am from a place where the air hangs heavy.
A blanket I can't throw off.
Holding me down, pinning my arms.
Giving me nowhere to look but up.

Earth and Breath

I remember hugging your neck.
Whiskers like sandpaper.
Giggles and trying to curl small enough to fit
Into the curve of your chest.
Hoping to be consumed whole.
One heartbeat, one person.

I remember swinging from hands
Held tight.
Twirling through time and space.
A lifeline, a connection.

I remember waiting to be tucked in,
Minutes dragging by like days.
Puppet shows in my doorway. You,
Directing Bert and Ernie to bid me
Good night.
Snug as a bug, sweet dreams.

I want you to know,
I tried to feel your cheeks, hold your fingers, tuck you in.
But they wouldn't let me.
I wanted to touch your chest, somehow
Restart your heart with my own.
One heartbeat, one person.
But they wouldn't let me.

A slamming shut, earth and breath separating us.

Funny to outgrow the things of childhood
But not the desire of childish things.
So what if I tuck myself in, hoping to glimpse you in my dreams?
So what if I thought I would somehow hear your voice,
Sense you in passing shadows?
So what? So what? So what?

I stamp my foot and hit my sides, but you still do not appear.
You are tucked in tight.
Far from me.
Snug as a bug, sweet dreams.

Homecoming

He said the birds don't sing in the city.
That I'm crazy to think I hear them.
But I do.

A whippoorwill calls when I lay myself down.
Its trill nothing short of a homecoming.

So clear that I can taste tilled soil on my tongue.
Hear the wind whipping through gnarled branches and mottled bark.
See a sycamore peeling its own skin back so to expose its insides to
    the sunlight.

Its call is earnest and eager, reminding me of the before.
A time where my hands were smooth as pebbles, my feet fast and
    friendly.
My breath easily found.

He comes every Sunday. This man who thinks I'm crazy for hearing
    a bird.
I don't remember his name.
Charles? David?
I may not know him, but I know the look in his eye.
I see my fingers. Gnarled and knotted like those trees in my mind.
My skin, translucent like sheets on the line.
I know the look of discomfort and of pity.
Of obligation.

I wonder if he is my child.
Born of my own body. Bearing my last name.

Strange to remember the rush of a creek bed but not the birth of a
    child.
Funny to recall the rhythm of rain on a tin roof but not the years
spent walking behind a boy.
Keeping him upright, fed, well-mannered.

I asked him his name before, but I don't remember what he said.
I don't want to ask again.
I saw the tears last time.
He must be someone special.
Does that make me someone special, too?

I may not know much but I feel much.
Like the need to be desired by a man,
His rough hands in my hair and on my tired back.
To feel the heat of a child, needing me more than anyone ever has.
I wish I could feel those hands, that heat, on me just one more time.
Before the whippoorwill stops calling.

To Have and to Hold

Like low hanging fruit
Frustratingly out of reach,
Our fingers fall short of feeling.
The past cannot be undone,
The mistakes are made.
What is left is putting pen to paper.
A condemning closure, in blue ink.

Counting Breaths

I tiptoe into your room
To count your breaths at night.
I examine your face to see the ways
It changed from yesterday.

I close my eyes and see our story.
A filmstrip projecting the past.
Images blurring together.
Smiles warm in the sunshine.
Splashes through puddles.
The moment I had to let go of your seat,
Your laughter flying behind as you pedaled against the wind.

We are allied in ways
Both temporary and permanent.
The filmstrip will one day unspool.
The ties between us will release.
We will become less than we are now.

But, tonight, I watch your chest rise and fall.
I smooth your blanket,
Run my fingers through your curls,
And listen for the sounds of sweet dreams.

Dripping

I can hear my mama, rocking in her chair,
"Ain't no stopping the flood once the levees break."
The blame drips from my limbs,
Guilt hangs heavy around my neck.

"Ain't no stopping the flood once the levees break."
The flood rages from my eyes, from my lips.
Guilt hangs heavy around my neck,
Comfort slips from my shaking fingers.

The flood rages from my eyes, from my lips.
He left when I was not ready for him to go.
Comfort slips from my shaking fingers.
My feet splash puddles where I see his face.

He left when I was not ready for him to go.
No shadow follows me.
My feet splash puddles where I see his face.
My chest rises and falls, rises and falls.

No shadow follows me.
Sleep no longer comes like before,
My chest rises and falls, rises and falls.
My bones feel larger than myself.

Sleep no longer comes like before.
My face hangs low with the weight of worry.
My bones feel larger than myself.
Everything stops at the end of the "before."

My face hangs low with the weight of worry.
The blame drips from my limbs,
Everything stops at the end of the "before."
I can still hear my mama, rocking in her chair.

On a June Night in 2000

We wore the night well.
A black dress fitting in all the right places.
The sizzle of summer making it too hot to dream.
Peeled labels, smoke swirls, giggles at everything and nothing.
We drained the stars from the sky and the bottles dry.
The crowns sat low on our heads.
Too heavy to remove, our hands distracted with other things.
Making plans to change the world.
Voices vowing to always remember our roots, our needs, each other.
We watched, together, as the orange swallowed the black above.
And the stars disappeared one by one.

Life Lessons

I can block and hide better than most.
I have learned not to leave my chin open, my core exposed, my legs
    straight.
I have learned that yelling makes it worse. That skin breaks but
    always heals.
It's immaturity. It's my failures, big and small. It's his birth family.
It's a lack of discipline and clear boundaries. It's the diagnosis.
But a diagnosis doesn't leave bruises.
It is an explanation without the hint of an answer.
I would guess most mothers don't drug their child to get them to sleep.
Only to be awakened by screaming as if limbs are being torn apart.
Sprinting to him, finding him in the fetal position in the corner of the
    bed.

Most nights my son doesn't want to go to sleep.
Who can blame him?
Most days I don't want to wake.
Who can blame me?

Some moments are happy, a fleeting image of the family
I created in my mind as a child,
Dreaming of white dresses and white fences.
But then the fidgeting begins, the name calling starts, the rage
    returns.

I dream of an escape, my feet moving upon sugary sands.
Waves roaring in my ears, wind tearing at my back.

A melody of peace and harmony.

I know I cannot go.
I would miss those hands, because they do not always cause injury.
Sometimes they hug and hold, soft and loving.
I would miss those eyes, because they do not always cry and glaze
    over.

Sometimes they crinkle with laughter, dark brown pools of delight.
I would miss that mouth, because it is not always telling me I am
   stupid.
Sometimes it gives kisses, while calling me a princess.

Instead of gritty dunes, my feet move upon hardwood to provide
   comfort.
My ears listen for warning signs of the rage to come.
My back holds the weight of this child, when he loves me and when
   he does not.

A different kind of melody, perhaps.
But it is mine to play.

The Welcome Mat

I'm trying to keep you safe,
You say as you slam the door.
Your voice a sound of home
I am no longer welcome to enter.

To Return to the Before
(For my father)

When I think of him walking out the
door, watching him move toward his
truck, looking at the strong back
I once stood high upon, ruling over my
kingdom six feet below me—

When I think of the embrace
that was too short, the words that danced on my
tongue but failed to pirouette off, the meal
that came in a cardboard box we shared moments
before, him happily talking and laughing about the day
as I stood distracted, feeding another—

When I think of the tone of the ring,
the tremble of my mother's vocal cords as she asked
to speak to someone else, the story brought by the
men in gray racing to beat the ten o'clock news—

When I think of the night without
sleep, the flood of tears at first that would not come,
the obstinate sting of denial, the way my body
felt heavier than my skin could bear, the muscles
failing to work to move me across a room,
the bones that felt larger than myself, the weight
of guilt strangling and pulling at my neck, too heavy
to carry alone but with no one else to share it—

When I think of the blur of days that followed,
the decisions to make, the hands to shake, the comfort to give
to others, the failure of my legs to carry me down the aisle
knowing the last aisle I had walked had been with him—

When I think of the mangled metal in the pictures I
have not seen, the details I do not know, the knowledge
that I called him to come, and he did so without a thought,
the me I was before and the stranger I am today—

When I think of my yearning to return to the "before,"
to rewind moments in time to a sunny day perched high
above the rest, that is when I clearly see him there,
the man just happy to be the shoulders
I stood upon.

The Middle

Our beginning is one I cannot remember.
Yet it resounds in me.
Clangs within my cage, beats within my gut.

I know we betrayed the unwritten rules.
Broke them in the difficult places.
But if we cared, it never showed.

So much of our moments I can remember.
The feeling of your stubble after a hard day's labor.
The yellow cups bursting from the earth you would pick for me
And never let grow.
Your tenor voice on a Sunday morning.

But for the life of me I can't remember our beginning.
We just always were.
Maybe that's enough to know.

I miss your strong hands on my stomach, pulling me close to you in
    the dark.
The way your eyes would cloud up when you were angry.
The direction you would tilt your head when you wanted something.
The quiet space shared between us.

On my way here, I saw the flags standing at half-mast.
I wonder if they feel as I do—
Yearning to be at the top again.
Not halted in the middle.

No, I may not know how we met.
But I have learned plenty of new lessons.
I know quiet is altogether different when there is no one to share it
    with.
Daffodils still die whether you pick them or not.
And six feet was never so long to travel as it is now.

Used to Be

"Can we forgive each other in the morning?"
His voice tore through the frustration.
A thawing of the words hanging above.
Those stuck between, unyielding.
Unforgiving.

To him, the morning is renewal.
A fresh start.
An opportunity to be seized.
How long had we been in the dark?
When did he begin to have faith in the light?

To me, every road seemed a dead end.
A foregone conclusion.
Branches smacking as we traversed the edge.
Cuts barely healing before the next open wound.
It never occurred to me to stop moving.
To either go backward or to separate along the path.
We stumbled along, bloody, aggrieved.
Bound up haphazardly.
Not wanting to admit defeat.
Too proud, coated in remorse.

Yet here he was.
Offering the idea of restoration.
Reconciliation.
A gentle nudging.
An effort to remember days spent under clear skies.
The sensation of laughter, of admiration, of brevity.
The used to be of us.

I turn, seeking out his features.
His curves and lines memorized over time.
Swollen scars matching my own.
A history nobody else should see.
One nobody else would understand.
I take his hand and we begin to walk back to the beginning.

A Mother's Love

They came in the spring and took
him from me. Saying I
was unfit and couldn't
care for him.
My life turned into a parade of
drug tests I couldn't afford,
counseling that did no good,
weekly one-hour visits supervised
by an overweight woman that probably
hits her kids too,
a judge that had it in for me
(probably bought off by the State),
and an appointed lawyer straight out of
law school who wanted me to admit to
abusing my kid so he
could make it to the golf course before 4:30.
I may not know much but I feel much and
there ain't a day goes by that I don't miss his smell,
his cry, his god-awful
need for attention all the damn time,
and the look on his face once the
welt would begin to rise.
His pain would cause him to curl up in my lap, and I
would hold him and say
"I'm sorry I'm a bad mommy"
and he,
bleeding and bruised,
would kiss my tears and tell me
I was the best mommy in the world.
And he was right.
They ain't never gonna see it
but he did
and that's all that matters to
me.

Exoneration

You beat the dog
But it continues to return,
Weaving through your legs,
Leaning against your heat.
You think you have won.
That you have dominated the beast.

It is merely waiting
For the moment to make its move
When you expect it least.

Tidal Wave

I played with fire.
Believing I would dance around it,
Daring it to burn my skin, singe my hair.
Not knowing it could cut through me,
Flames licking the scars on my belly,
Consuming my wringing hands.
I drop to my knees, my throat constricts.
I pull to the position I know best.
The one used in the womb of my mother.
Grief runs over me, a tidal wave.
I wanted your hands on my body.
Tangling my hair, pulling me around you.
Your lips tasting my fingertips.
Alone is my new domicile.
Where I live,
Scratching at the door of yesterday.
Begging the memories of bedsheets,
The feel of you against me,
To wash away with the shifting sand.
Whatever you needed me to be,
The perfect woman. The best lover.
I could have been that for you.
Now I see only your back,
Choosing her.
Leaving me to love you,
As I am dragged beneath the surface.

Hands

There is constant noise, like the hum of a life lived downtown.
The machine makes a soft, shooshy sound every few seconds.
It is connected to a cord like the one I use to charge my iPhone.
I could walk over and unplug it
As easily as I do the now neglected vacuum cleaner.
But then the alarms would toll, and the numbers would turn from
   green to red—
A Christmas tree, a stoplight.
I have not tried to unplug it. You're welcome.
The nurses buzz you up and down, as they poke and prod you from
   scalp to toe.
Over your right shoulder is a flashing monitor.
It draws the attention of the scampering nurses.
The sedation drug, thick and white,
Is injected through the plastic tube running into your nose.
The doctors come in, clicking and clacking notes on the keyboard to
   your left.
They use a scanner, the kind I like to use at Target,
To scan your bracelet, your identity reduced to a plastic ring.
They key in updates (very few), changes (none),
Modifications they make with drugs for pain (a lot).
They tell me it was lucky you qualified for a feeding tube in your nose
Instead of a permanent one in your gut. Small victories.
Sometimes, your fingers twitch.
You even raise your hand and I think you are coming back.
Like I have been waiting for you at our table in the coffee shop.
I see you breeze through the door; you lift your fingers to wave
But then you return to the car. A forgotten wallet.
You come and you go.
I ready myself to call the nurse. But your eyes never open.
They say it is a nerve causing your movement,
Not anything you are willing your hand to do.
I remember when we were home, your back to me in bed.
You always fell asleep first.

I would turn out the light (you hate that light) and place my hand on
   your back.
A reminder of growing up in church.
When someone was ill, or hurting,
We would approach the altar, surrounding them.
Heat from our bodies, muffled voices, stinging tears.
Some would kneel, others would stand.
We would lay hands on the afflicted person.
If we could not reach them, we would lay hands on the person
   next to us,
Links in a chain.
Our voices would raise as one, crying for a remedy from God.
Lilts and falls, pauses and continuances.
Maybe I should have done more of that for you.
Instead, I sit in this chair, thinking of our hands,
The good they used to do and the time we used to waste.

Intersection

Jesus stares at me from the sign
Stuck haphazardly in the dirt.
Something to look at while I wait for lights to change.
Green, yellow, red.
The blood drips
drips
drips.
Seeping from holes in wrists and ankles.
The left turn signal clicks
clicks
clicks.
"He sacrificed for you!"
"Remember His pain!"
"Your existence is because of Him!"
These words are the undercurrent of my life.
A constant reminder of a woman's worth.
I sit here, waiting for the green light.
Wondering how long I must repay a sacrifice
I never asked to be made.

Bound

I am afraid
Of things I cannot forget.
What I did,
I did for you.
For us.
My only thoughts,
Protect.
Preserve.
Survive.
And yet.
You did not come back to me.
I am afraid
You have forgotten me.
Or worse,
You never thought of me.
That this was fiction.
A novel with an ending foreseen by all
But me.
I am afraid
I will only see you behind closed eyes.
In my dreams.
Where I cannot feel the pressure
Of your hips on mine.
I need your voice,
Your eyes penetrating mine.
Our unspoken words floating through
The space between.
I am afraid of too many things
So, I sleep all day.
Waiting for you.
Hazy flashes only to be replaced
With the empty hours I am awake.
There is no path forward for me.
No pulling myself up
By the ties that bind.
I am afraid.
Cut me loose.

Deliverance

I never wanted this.
To be someone you admired.
To carry the weight of that responsibility.
The way your eyes glaze over when they glance my way.
Like I'm your savior, the one to lead you to the light.
You should not depend on me.
You should not want more than I can give.
It is unfair.
It is stupid.
It is misplaced.
I don't know the way.
If I did, I would go alone.
I would leave you behind.
And I would forget you ever haunted me.

Soliloquy

"You're a glutton for punishment," you once said
To a crowded room.
Faces smiling politely,
Heads nodding.
No one noticing as
You removed the lungs from my chest.

You talked while I collapsed
Into a ball of organs.
My bones disappeared long ago
When you needed to pick clean your teeth.

June

I heard her say,
"Weak men, they do make the world go round."
Fury, disappointment, resentment
Rolled, twisted, and catapulted
From her tongue.
When the past follows you,
Ripping and scratching for your attention,
Can there be a future?
The screams for justice grow too loud to ignore.
Some may call it a poor choice,
But they are part of the problem,
Asking the wrong questions and
Casting misplaced judgment,
When she never had a choice at all.

Keeper of Things

He said he doesn't put much stock in dreams.
That's a good thing, I think to myself.
A wife ought to be dreaming about the one she wakes up next to,
Day in and day out.
The one whose clothes she cleans, whose babies she's birthed.

Yet it's you who visits me when my eyes are at rest.
When they are not seeking out stains to treat,
Children to keep upright,
Water that's reached boiling.
When they can rest easy and stop searching, that's when I see you.
The curve of your cheek, the trill in your laughter,
The warmth of your core.
I see, I hear, I feel,
I remember.
I remember what it is like to smile so much it hurts.
To feel breath catch in my own body because your hand
Secretly met mine.
To come undone at the lifting up of your lips into a half smile.

But I also remember vows given at the front of a stifling church.
Children calling "Mommy" hundreds of times a day,
Needing nothing and everything all at the same time.
A love, however stale, that is consistent and well intentioned.

In the mornings the person I could have been,
The passion I could have experienced,
Dissipates under the weight of babies on hips,
Of the same lips on mine before the door slams shut.

I bet you think it was easy.
This choice I made.
To honor promises given,
To try to reconcile betrayal,
To be everything to those who clamor for my tired affection,
My despondent attention,
My constant looking past them for you.

You wouldn't recognize my lips that seldom form a smile,
The evenness of my breath,
The limp touch of my hands.
I grieve who I was in your arms.
I fear never knowing that girl again
Except for those hours we meet in my dreams.
There, I am vibrant, renewed, wanted for who I am
Not just for what I can do for someone else.
I am loved. I am seen. I am heard.
Yes, I remember.

Vessel

I assume the position.
In my mind, I see myself—
Forehead on knees, arms wrapped tight
Around slender shins.
I visualize myself atop a high shelf,
A porcelain doll with china hands, feet, and head,
Thin cracks running through its translucence,
The stuffing of the body lumpy and uneven.
Sometimes I tuck away in the back of a dark closet,
Next to sticky spiderwebs and scratchy wool coats.
I hum, I count, I replay funny videos in my brain.
The dog floating on the pool noodles across the swimming pool.
The cat blocking the passengers as they leave the subway—
Refusing to yield its space on the sidewalk.
Stubborn and sure of who it is and what it wants.
I pretend not to feel your tongue like sandpaper,
Your prowling hands seeking warmth and wetness.
My body handing it to you, a betrayal.
I wish to be cold and limp, dry as a bone.
I wish to be anyone else, anywhere else.
To be that forgotten doll, the neglected coats.
Not the person turned inside out by you.

Seasonality

It is now spring.
The rain has come and gone.
I dig my toes in the dirt.
It's soft like my insides.
The change in seasons has not changed our distance.
The lines on my face have multiplied since we last met.
You're fine.
I'm fine.
So many words I want to say,
Or stammer,
Your direction.
But the courage,
The opportunity,
Never arrives.
I watch an earthworm
Stick its head (or tail?)
Out of the brown beneath me.
The path it takes, over clumps,
Through tunnels,
Does it know where it is going?
Feeling around in the dark.
Trying to find its way,
Only to be washed away by the next storm.
I dream about you.
Your face clearly in focus.
Your hand on my cheek,
So very real to me.
I know I need to pull myself together.
To forget these scars.
Yet, I cannot see the end of this.
These nighttime visits
Always bring a hangover in the morning.
Eyes squinting, mouth dry,

Drunk from being in your presence.
I wish things could have been different.
This impossibility that is us.
I wish I wasn't like this earthworm.
Constantly moving on top of this Kentucky soil,
Never quite knowing how to find my way home.
And forever fearing the fall of rain.